WATER

LOOK

AWAY

ALSO BY BOB HICOK

Red Rover Red Rover

Hold

Sex & Love &

Elegy Owed

Words for Empty and Words for Full

This Clumsy Living

Insomnia Diary

Animal Soul

Plus Shipping

The Legend of Light

WATER

LOOK

AWAY

BOB HICOK

COPPER CANYON PRESS
PORT TOWNSEND, WASHINGTON

Cover design by Phil Kovacevich

Copper Canyon Press is in residence at Fort Worden State Park in Port
Townsend, Washington, under the auspices of Centrum. Centrum is
a gathering place for artists and creative thinkers from around the
world, students of all ages and backgrounds, and audiences seeking
extraordinary cultural enrichment.

LIBRARY OF CONGRESS CATALOGING-IN-PUBLICATION DATA
Names: Hicok, Bob, 1960- author.
Title: Water look away / Bob Hicok.
Description: Port Townsend, Washington : Copper Canyon Press, [2023] |
Summary: "A new collection of poems by Bob Hicok"—
Provided by publisher.
Identifiers: LCCN 2022057807 (print) | LCCN 2022057808 (ebook) |
ISBN 9781556596506 (paperback) | ISBN 9781619322745 (epub)
Subjects: LCGFT: Poetry.
Classification: LCC PS3558.I28 W37 2023 (print) |
LCC PS3558.I28 (ebook) | DDC 811/.54—dc23/eng/20221205
LC record available at https://lccn.loc.gov/2022057807
LC ebook record available at https://lccn.loc.gov/2022057808

9 8 7 6 5 4 3 2 FIRST PRINTING

COPPER CANYON PRESS
Post Office Box 271
Port Townsend, Washington 98368
www.coppercanyonpress.org

for Eve

*One of the first signs of the beginnings of
understanding is the wish to die.*

FRANZ KAFKA

*The strongest principle of growth lies in
human choice.*

GEORGE ELIOT

*And the things you can't remember
tell the things you can't forget
that history puts a saint in every dream.*

TOM WAITS

CONTENTS

Welcome Home   3

Last Days of Rome   4

The Arrival   5

Ntre or Nrtre?   7

The Opening   8

Birds of a Feather   9

Diagnosis   10

Writer, Heal Thyself   12

Bio on the Head of a Pin   13

A Field of Plume Grass   14

Snow Globe   15

Holding Breaking Close   16

Marriage   18

A Man Can Be an Arrow If He Can Find a Bow   19

The Birth of Shorthand   20

The Difference between Wanting to Be and Being   21

Weight   22

Wealth   24

The Long Wish   26

An Accounting   27

A Sense of Everything Not Written Down   29

Seeing Someone Else's Seeing Is Believing   31

Physical   32

The New Tense   33

Knowing   34

Eden (Need)   36

For Some Reason Always in the Car   38

Apology as Burial (Hers)   39

Amends   40

The Last Time   41

Triangulation   44

The Meet-Cute (Actual, with Redaction)   45

Three Revolutions around the Planet of the Same Idea   47

Housekeeping   48

Housekeeping   50

Twined   51

Two Steps Forward, One Off a Cliff   52

Apology as Promises (His)   53

Self-Critique   54

A Woman in Motion   55

He Explains   56

Stephanie   57

Ornithology   58

Solitude, a Math Problem   60

What from the Outside Seems Whim from the Inside
Goes by *Avalanche*   62

Space Travel   64

Real Love   65

The Meet-Cute (a Pagedream)   66

Now We're Not Getting Somewhere   70

A Natural Theory of Suicide   72

Used Book, Omen   74

Did She Leave a Suicide Image?   76

A Recipe   78

Gone   79

Stride for Stride   80

About the Author   82

WATER

LOOK

AWAY

Welcome Home

In the basement. An
extension cord. Passed
through a hole. He'd
bored. In a joist. Which
means she. Knew. That
no pipe would. Hold. Under
or technically. Above
her. Weight. The
beauty. Of the
noose. Suggested she
had. Googled "how to
hang. Oneself with. An
extension. Cord." Perfect.
Holding his wife. Up by
bear-hugging her. Calves, he
listened for. Breath for. Ten
minutes. To this night he
dreams. That in-. Rush of.
Air. Surprised it. Wasn't
him and. Jealous she got.
There first.

Last Days of Rome

She lights matches to see the thoughts
of gasoline.

The circling of a tribe of vultures
in his eyes.

Her studio flooded, his mouth full of bees.

Otherwise they need milk, eggs.

The Arrival

Drinks with friends.
She came with a woman who vibrated
at the frequency of "a Plank
in Reason, broke."
With everyone else at the table
in a race to kill silence, their hush
a copse. After a while
she drew a hawk on her wrist
in blue ink. The hawk
is taking your pulse, he said.
She drew a rabbit on his
and warned that his wrist
should run from hers. On a napkin
she wrote, *I am afraid of the switchblades*
in faces trying to be happy.
An antidote came to him—
a metal roof, rain—
but when he tried to draw
this peace, his rain
looked like bullets and his house
reminded her of a sat-on hat.
She drew a better house
for them, a safer rain.
How do you translate eyes,
a problem no language

has solved: looking at her
was like hearing a coyote
at night. He woke up.

Ntre or Nrtre?

Stole a setof wtrcolor paintz, a kidz set
at elvn and the rght feelng feel
of her fvrite red shrt slpped over her
whnevr she mde bleedng sun-swirls
and rose-blobz and bonz bonz bonz in pilz
aftr fndng a strved dog in the woodz
tied to a tree, poordog poortree. The rnning
of evrythng twrd else, othr, mde her hnst
and bad at mths: *How mny applz
dos Jnny hve? Nne,* she wrote at twlv
whn the tst askd. *Jnny'z dead.*

The Opening

Honesty can never make it to the end of itself.
An idea can sound right because it is sharp
on two or three sides, he thinks,
though not necessarily true. The music
of conviction, not the weight of a heart
on a scale. Hollow, in other words,
like having only clouds
for emotions or kissing like ash.
What if the past never wanted me
and I have been the guest
a friend asked along, the one
not invited by the host?
There he is again, thinking
of his voice as a stenographer taking down
the king one word at a time. King
of what? Holding a barrel
to his temple but not being able to finish
the thought? I never told God
I was sorry for being sorry
the world exists. I assumed God feels
the same way too.

Birds of a Feather

His mother, knowing his high school
had to accept whatever she wrote,
as long as she signed whatever she wrote,
wrote a note for an absence:

My son is sugar and would have melted in the rain.

On the way to school he replaced *sugar*
with *sad* to keep his mother from lying,
and told his wife before they were married,
before they had so much as traded books,
that some days he could not get out of bed
for years. Do

they look like this, she said of the yeardays,
and pressed an eye to the hole in her fist.

Diagnosis

Left cheek against the window of December,

the cool his career for an hour, then right,

then nose and chin, knowing he cannot stir

himself to do any of the things technically

he could do—kiss an orange, burn his passport,

buy roses and give them to daisies—

the cold dulling the knife of having

to move and/or breathe and/or try

to bite the glass or eat the gray sky

of his mind in its locked room

chain-smoking for days, Does it not seem to you

gray is the only real weather

I have ever been, he asks himself and says,

Leave me out of this hole your life

is the shovel of, a well that never

reaches water.

Writer, Heal Thyself

But notice

the thread

down the side

of that well

(imagination): How

do you smoke chains?

and begin

to climb

Bio on the Head of a Pin

While others were jumping rope,
keeping time before blood
tracked their underwear down,
she gathered stray bones into an animal
Linnaeus would have named
More,

rabbit skull, crow wings, possum tail, moonlight,
a recipe of sheddings that shamed the imagination
of god.

A Field of Plume Grass

Reading *The Life of a Stupid Man,* beyond
the writing, he likes the size of the book,
which is about the size of his hand;
it recommends modesty to anyone who holds it.
With Akutagawa he sees a window hovering
above a mountain, implying a house, a window
that ripens to a cloud every time he reaches
to open it. Books have the good manners
to be indifferent to us unconditionally.
Imagine that being is a piece of paper
folded and folded to the density of a quasar
and then a whisper comes and finds its center,
where it is written, Behold, Be hold, Be held:
every book is a challenge to embrace.
Perhaps *offer* has less of the pollution
of critique: every story is an offer to embrace.
The book: a pocket that fits his pocket, a carrying
he carries, a reminder to care for every vessel
he will touch or be. Black cover, white text:
an inversion of the country inside,
where words cover their mouths and paper burns
without turning into his future: ash.

Snow Globe

Her with a book and him with her with a book
and with a book himself, him reading her reading
her book and reading his book too, the moon
reading them both and the snow and the snow
reading the moon and the trees and the trees
are maples and cedars and reading too, the dog
reading sleep and the fire reading the end
of time without telling how the story
of endings ends, her reading his breath
reading her breath reading the wind
turning the shadows of the pages of the trees.

Holding Breaking Close

She had a friend once she watched
lie belly down for hours on a rock
with her head sticking out
above the churn and smash
of the Atlantic, who finally sat up
and looked blasted out of her life,
a piece of broken glass to be with
except then. She told him she had never

wanted to kiss anyone more, and he wanted
to kiss the friend too, tired of arguing
in the dark and grateful
for the neutral ground of the story
of this opened face. She put her head

on his stomach and wondered
if they had just decided to live together
apart or apart together, keeping to herself
that she had kissed the woman then, later,
often, saying instead she was curious
if water in the ocean thought of itself
differently from water in our lips,
or was it all the same slow flowing,
and wouldn't it be great to ask water
if leaving felt the same to it
as coming home, since it was always

doing both, and have water look away
and think for a hundred years
before answering.

Marriage

Do you take
(no

give.) Do
you give

(no
hold.) Do
you hold

(no
river.) Do
you river

(yes I river
this man/woman
into/as
my breath.)

A Man Can Be an Arrow If He Can Find a Bow

He wants to go and be erased.
Atby the sea. Atby a dream
in which he is a plant
that can walk, that burrows
into the ground after a woman
wearing a white shirt and black skirt
peels back the floorboards
and holds open his escape.
Not walk, not slither, something
between, though combined,
one option is *wither*
and it is anything but a decay,
a loss, this door of a woman,
a dream, a sea. All of this paper
on which he has written
all of the reasons
for this leaving
and none of them right
or elegant or sharp enough
to peel back his skin.
What do bones care about the reasons
for bones? The desire
an extra rib. The word *desire*
too timid: think *foundry*
or the sun eating itself
into light.

The Birth of Shorthand

Their first Halloween she went
to a party as Frida Kahlo's unibrow.
Will you be Rivera's infidelity,
she begged, putting aside how.
The whole night she said Zapata
and nothing else. He went
as Camus's jealousy of Sartre.
How could anyone have known, she asked
on the way home, skipping backward
ahead of his shrug. I thought
the intensity of my teeth
would do the trick. Intensity
isn't articulate, she said,
it can only hum or scream.
A week later, when she hadn't
left her room for two days,
he slipped a note in, Hum
or scream? Yes came back.

The Difference between Wanting to Be and Being

After they fucked against a wall, she ran away
and back with red paint, a brush, painted a bed
on the wall and below it the word *Bower*
so people would ask and she could say nothing
in a different way than otherwise she might have.

Weight

The desire for substance.
As in coffee.
They have coffee
with both sets of hands
around blue cups. Clay
the substance of cups. The idea
of the cup the mother
of the substance of cups. Or
so we say, he says
in and to his brain,
but what of loving
the prayer of her hands
around the cup: is there a ghost
somewhere of that feeling, an ur-urge
that I am the poor child of?
How unlikely
she is thinking the same.
What are you thinking,
he asks. She looks up
and across the steam.
That if you left
I would cut the holeshape
of you in our bed
and fill it with water
and touch the shore

of you at night.
That is what he imagines.
What she really says:
Cinnamon in the coffee
was a good idea.
Because they are her words
they taste like sugar and salt.

Wealth

The sun pulls up a chair.
She remembers music
skimming across a lake,
touching July, an oboe
building a house in the air.

Taking a break
from how busy she's been
wanting to die
to engage the sky
on its own terms, she is clear,
cloudless, bounded by trees
on either side and nothing
when she looks up
and closes her eyes.

She couldn't survive
without the option
to not: hope is knife,
noose, the rattle of pills
in her heart, where cops
and love can't touch them,
where to erase, leave no trace,
is the only proof
of self and self-

possession: "I am empty
but the zero is mine."

The Long Wish

Sitting in a meadow with grass
after a hundred years
of stillness, maybe
I would be grass
he thinks, thinks a woman
is coming to stand behind him,
kiss the top of his head,
let her hair fall,
reside over his face
as a gate between the meadow
and his looking and the air
and his breathing and infinity
and wanting to ask it, Do you too
get tired of yourself?

An Accounting

Her affair was first
a sail raised on a mast
and then the storm
that broke the sail in two
but left the mast unharmed.

Too complicated.

Her affair was first
his fault for leaving her
alone with him in the same room
with his mind down the well
of books for years.

Too empty.

Her affair was first
an accident second a parachute
third an étude for left hand
and orgasm fourth a knife
in the future
fifth a garroting
of the past sixth
a garroting of the past
seventh a garroting
of the past eighth

two women
holding hands
under a table.

A Sense of Everything Not Written Down

It will be worth it
the rest of his life, any amount
of whining from Kafka
for "The *ah*, released from the sentence,
flew off like a ball on the meadow."
Miserable on Tuesday miserable
on Thursday: is that not the metronome
of every diary?
But he stuck with it,
the Tuesdays and Thursdays,
in another man's
and the diary
he did not write, an infinity: the diaries
he did not write. Reading with the moon
at the table. Wondering why
he does not cry, wanting his face
to rust. The reflex to think
in threes: I love peaches, I love bones
in the crooks of trees, I love rain
falling up, missing heaven.
Waiting.
The migraines of clocks.
The Alzheimer's of seasons.
The feeling his shadow
looks the other way when he steps

into the sun.
Waiting for a ball on the meadow
of his heart.

Seeing Someone Else's Seeing Is Believing

A room with blocks. On a wall, a portion of the floor.
Brightly colored spheres and squares and swirls
of paint in similar and different colors
around and under the blocks. The room otherwise black
except for a light pointed at the blocks and swirls
that changes into different animal shinings
as a transparent wheel of various colors
turns in front of the light. The light and the wheel
changing red blocks and swirls to blue
for example and back: the biology of color
and mood alive in a room as quiet as the hinge
of a buried casket except for the whirring
of the turning of the motor that moves the wheel.
A Hockney. They loved this room instantly
and married it to their kissing of what the world is
and should be. Since jump, one, the other would turn
and ask, *Do you like that house, that blue car,*
that dress, that kind of fire in an oboe's mouth,
and know the answer before the asking
as certainly as rain rarely falls up. Love:
one aesthetic looking the other in the eye.

Physical

His ear sewn to her chest.
A pilgrim wing above her heart.
Foghorn in her blood,
the postage of wind.
Any two can hold hands, spleens, arsons:
the trick is frontal lobes,
breath.

The New Tense

Runninged to the toilet,
a spot of then a lot
of blood, cryinged on knees
then cryinged on knees
with a bucket then cryinged
curled naked in the tub,
"Stay out" all night she said
behind locked door: a memory
constantly having the child
of itself, everborn past.

(They'd stopped reaching
for condoms in Paris, by London
threw them out, by Amsterdam:
she felt a dream in her womb.)

The scythes of people saying
"You'll try again" and trying again
and failing to stop people
from sighing for years,
his mother yesterday,
her hand on his: At least
you have each other.

How she heard it:
You have each other least.

Knowing

Three years after her miscarriage
and still pretending. For him. For him.
For her. For her. For them. Pretending
walking talking dreaming fucking.
Pretending best to herself
until the fleshwhisper again,
the thumpalina.
Until she felt her body growing
to serve. To chalice.
And didn't want her flesh
to be a dress life wore
only to shed. Afraid
of the milk pulse, the night crawl,
that the song "mommommom"
would kill her name,
she drove alone across town
with a friend, alone
within and without herself,
and went alone into a room
with two kind and focused women
and a machine that shouted air
and came out resumed
and differently the same
as she went in. She finally knew
that the vine that grew within her

craved a different kind of life
than tiny sighs, is how she'd put it
a month later in a letter to him
sealed in two envelopes and mailed
from their home to their home.
But that day, she cried away from the clinic
with her head against
the cool October window
on the way to "anywhere that's nowhere,"
she told her friend, cried like a tornado
would cry if cut in half.
But only with her left eye.

Eden (Need)

Winding path down
to shore. He knew the number of steps then.
Little metal table and chairs to the right
halfway down, good for coffee, for staring
at the curve of the earth where lake and sky
pretended to be each other, for writing of her dreams
as she dreamed them: they compared the real
to the built and she would decide whose head
deserved a kiss. Dream of the concertina torso,
actual music of breath (his). A woman who felt the pain
of an anvil with every stroke (his). A train
that refused to move, a vehicle of *no,*
mountains and rivers running by, in a hurry
to be mortal (hers). They would walk and swim
at dawn and noon and walk and swim and make love
surrounded by the lips of dark water. Drives
to other beaches and small towns with small stores
with fewer items than he thought people
could survive on without boredom forcing them
to leave notes on tables to their past, *I love you
but you are a broken arrow.* He was good at being wrong,
came to love the single jar of peanut butter
on the shelf, the choice between tomato soup
and no soup reminding him to thank his hands
for touching her face. It was this simple:
the woman who checked them in

took his sorrow. Took it without asking
when they arrived and gave it back
when they left, its appetite unharmed, its moan
as cello-deep as before. Years of this absolution
and then it was gone. The inn sold
without anyone asking, Are you done with the rituals
that have smoothed your bones? They tried
other inns and hotels but it felt as if the lake
itself had burned down. A few years later,
he had a character say of her sorrow,
There is a little woman in me
who grinds and eats her own teeth.
The story won a prize, was absorbed
by the imagination of an era, he was asked about it
and answered and thanked people and smiled,
even though it was the most violent story
he ever wrote. In another story, he gave that woman
an apple tree to apologize for pushing his mouth
through hers, ruining her story into his,
as that character didn't feel that way
about her sorrow at all. *There is a little dog in me*
waiting for the sound of a car in the drive.
Only his wife recognized that he was trying
to hate the sky when this woman got in his way.
You owe her more than an apple tree,
she said one night as she walked to her room.
At that point they were speaking to each other
almost solely by leaving dirty dishes in the sink.

For Some Reason Always in the Car

She asks
he says
I do not
think about
it any
more. She

asks he
says I
do not think
about it
any more.
She asks he

says I
do not
think about
it any
more than
I have
to. (A

penny for
your thoughts

of guns.)

Apology as Burial (Hers)

I painted the last you two mirrors
at a slight angle to each other would see
to help you stand where infinity is trying
to speak to us.

Under that I painted me going down on her
and painted over that in black and painted over that
in sky and painted over that in blood to bury alive
how I killed you to get even with you needing me
to need you too much.

Under that I painted water shattering at the top
into discrete plummetings that live as ribbons
and bowls and sighs and wombs torn apart
as they dive and knit at the bottom of the falls
back into the common flowing that we are.

Whatever you want me to paint
beneath that, I will find a way under
for you, I owe you that,
woe you that, love you
still.

Amends

He watches his wife folding the shirt
he was wearing when he kissed another woman
on the same bridge he crossed with her
in a hurry to catch a ferry to an island
where a man was kept prisoner for kissing
a queen. We should each burn the last thing
we have touched, he says, his hand
on his heart. She notices this and says,
Without that you will be hollow.
I have been hollow with it, he thinks better
of saying but says something close:
It is the one city my blood refuses to touch.

The Last Time

The opening of her biggest show.

Manhattan wanted to adore

by spending. A series

of reverse portraits, faces

as seen from the faceless inside

out, because she knew

we are nowhere certain

in mind how our looking

looks. And other people as mirrors

are so bad and breakable, too busy

trying to see us seeing them

to show us ourselves seeing

ourselves. A hiving night. Thrum of talking/

heat/champagne, the feeling of feeling

a throng of people believe

they are in the right room

at the right time, surfing the zeitgeist,

and being terrified of their mouths,

the cannibalizing chatter

of hipness. In that slaughter, he looked over

and saw her in a second of quiet,

everyone briefly cleared away,

and was reminded of a photo

of a fawn and mountain lion cub

found curled together under a desk

in an office on the edge of a forest fire:

the soft oblivion

of her face. Be careful what you wish for. Wish

for being careful. He tried

to throw his eyes across the room, but another wave

of adoration broke. Coming to her he whispered,

Too bad my machete

is at the cleaners. She took his hand, almost

broke it.

Triangulation

A man a woman a woman at a table.
A woman a man a woman at sea.
A woman a woman a man throwing horseshoes.
As if rain has been reading their diaries.
As if the dead body in Bruegel under a sheet is sleeping.
As if halos exist on their own.
As if a hat forgotten in a taxi makes it to Paris after all.
As if putting one thing next to another is a disguise.
As if everyone lives until photographs forget us.
A man a woman a woman doing a crossword.
Word for "Aligns the chakras."
Word for "Churchill thought she was a cigar."
Word for "No one gets what they want everyone tries."
Word for "God wonders who god is and looks up."
Word for "She loves she, she loves she, he loves they."
A man a woman a woman in bed.
A woman a man a woman in bed.
A woman a woman a man in bed.
A woman a woman in bed. A man
floats between two islands
touching one, touching the other
with the touch of one, then the other.
As if a man is an introduction.
As if a man is as if.

The Meet-Cute (Actual, with Redaction)

You have a zit.

(He touches his nose.) It makes me feel seventeen.

God I remember waking to a zit and thinking my life was over.

Did you like popping them?

Yes. Especially earlobe zits. The sound was purifying, like confession without the priest or the sin.

The vile expelled.

Yes. What's your name?

_____. What's yours?

Anna.

That's a beautiful name. You are the same forward as back.

Are you saying I'm boring?

No. I think I'm saying palindromes are words that have figured something out and can't help telling the truth, even if you spin them around to confuse them.

I like that.

Me too. It makes me think of piñatas, of spinning and smashing.

That's all there is.

That's all there is.

Three Revolutions around the Planet of the Same Idea

1

I was born a woman, he thinks, jiggling his breasts
in the mirror and imagining his penis unfolding
into labia and flying as a monarch to Mexico
a day later when his wife touches lightness awake
in him.

2

In other words, biology has made men double
and not quite whole is what you're saying,
the interviewer asked, not noticing his brain
was floating just outside the window, looking back
at them both and laughing at himself.

3

"A woman is a homecoming for a man; a man
a different country for a woman." For an hour
he squints at that sentence, sips coffee, hates
the novel and his life so far, tries again.
"For a man a woman is the oldest mirror;
for a woman a man is Phil if his name is Phil."

Housekeeping

Did she read the derailment possessively,
from the inside out, he wonders back into time.
Opens the novel: the train, the bridge, the ice,
the night, the black, and goes into the water
with the men lowered on ropes, loses his breath
inside their erasure from view, returns without her
every time, an emptiness like a hymn
sung backward, away from god.

Did she read the passage aloud? Did she read
the passage aloud as if it were fire
after a cold rain? Did she read the passage aloud
as if burying the seed of what she wanted
in her throat? Did she read the passage aloud
to give him the premonition to leave her be,
to not bother coming in after her undering?
Did she read the passage aloud
to put an ax in the hand of a tree,
to practice repairing her death into art?

He looks at the shape of her sitting on the couch.
It did not die. Her shirts and skirts did not.
Her saying, That would be enough eternity for me,
of the possible glide of the train through water
before settling, versus going to the bottom
straightaway, did not die. When is a train

a wing? When he closes his eyes. Sees her face
in the last car, turning away.

Housekeeping

Every time she read of the train
going off the bridge in the book

she'd read to death (duct-taped
spine, much of the breath

of her eyes caught in its pages),
she wondered if her reflection

would have looked at her
from the other side and brought

a finger to its lips, if hush
isn't the answer to everything.

Twined

Maybe a root flows lips to nipples and *After,*
she lived as balloon, a cut string
in their kiss, underground. *the slightest breeze*
removing her from her own eyes
and conversation. There always was this blood tug
Like a premonition that her shadow would be gone
come morning, when he so much as brushed,
let alone suckled, *her feelings had given up*
on words like an echo of the sun's heart
falling through her. *and run loose, animals*
in a zoo of exploded cages. In that way, a man
is a practice child *Filling a body*
with ears in one painting, and not to be listened to
when he wants to turn his toys into war.
she wouldn't let him look at the hollow
of her listening for breath. Some things
are too personal, *For a person to live*
sharpened to severing where a lover
there can't be a wish for air where blood
belongs. or even the self needs to hold them.

Two Steps Forward, One Off a Cliff

Admitting teaches them what not to admit
and what ritual can do to save them.
By this equation they arrive at burning
love letters from other people together
in the garden. If we read them once
we will never stop reading them twice
never stop reading an nth time
while eating touching dreaming of never
having lived. Lighter fluid. A match.
A suicide note slipped among his, a draft:
"I am tired of asking existence to notice
how much I worry about its shape and breath,"
everything crossed out except "I am tired."
A complicated smoke: the smoke of memory
for both the smoke of oblivion for both
the smoke of what do we do now
that we are looking at each other
and wondering, Are you writing a letter
with the smoke of your thoughts
to someone you love more
differently than me?

Apology as Promises (His)

I will put my mouth in a jar
under the sea. Read the faces of women
who read tea leaves. Stab my cock
with a tombstone. Donate my body
to intuition. Walk under the umbrella
of your shadow. I will sew your paintings
to my eyes. Bring each of your tears
a jaguar. Take the name of your sorrow
as my own. Eat a crutch, limp and all.
Will only speak when the moon
speaks to me. Bury a crib
for every child your womb was right
to refuse. The ash of my hand
will hold the bones of yours.

Self-Critique

The drama of beauty
more natural than the drama of plot.

A herd of elk in a church, a skinned woman
sipping tea: a painting
is its own proof.

But reading this in a book—

"Hearing herself in the rain, she grew quieter
as the days went on, convinced her thoughts
were the source of the flood"—

it is natural to put the book over your eyes
like a tent or throw it across the room,
certain no life would take this shape
or if it did, this girl would wear a dress
of lilacs, not roses, have brown hair
instead of black, and one day walk off
and never be heard from again, not buy
a little house and paint the door red, he thinks

as he burns half a year's work, one page at a time,
three pages alone for the door
and red, speculating on the nature of blood,
if it remembers, if it has ears.

A Woman in Motion

Who still comes home
with skinned knees at 32, rust
in pocket and eyes
full of shorebruises,
the beatings of waves
arriving endlessly to fail
at embrace?
Everyone
she was and then
some.

He Explains

To flow . . . enter into and become . . . a thrust
that turns to water, a softening hard . . . to make
a face of our faces . . . a child would see the future
with our eyes.

She nods like someone pretending to dowse.

When it's her turn she says shrug, says closed eyes
and rocking, finally: *I won't be responsible*
for another scream.

He watches a man pick up his dog's shit.
Thinking it's impossible they haven't talked
about children, he remembers that the atom bomb
exists, that oops is a muse.

We'll be fine, he says to her, the man, the dog,
the muse, the poop.

None of them say anything back.

Stephanie

Speaking through a seawall
wind, screaming against its one oath, her hand
reaching through the tempesting of the other her's
black hair, as if goodbye, as if leaving
as many fingerprints on her lips as possible,
giving maybe one maybe the chance to maybe remain,
leaning in, this time mouth to ear, this time
as a tree to another tree raised as children
by the same storms, the same prevailing romance
of atoms holding hands and letting go, leaning in
and setting a bit of wet breath free
though speechless, kissless, just holding there,
dwelling as if fruit, leaf, as if of all the falls,
this one lasting, last

Ornithology

Reasons are fun
to pretend reasonable. It is
the same bird. It is the same bird
because he wants it to be. It is
the same bird because he wants today
as yesterday as always to be the same.
It is the same pileated woodpecker
brushing its beak against the window.
Same infatuation with the image
of itself. A writer bird, he writes
the same as he wrote, Her vagina
green in spring, by fall
shedding leaves. Same flying away
and coming back to the same ledge
of the same house of the same looking
of things a certain way. Even
a burned-down house is a home,
once your eyes sit among the ashes
and take a load off, once you have breathed
the shape of ruin. The same feeling
that he has only ever seen the movie
of his face in the mirror.
How to run around the self to see
the bones behind? At least the bird
tries. Flies. Who is insane, the man

who thinks he is a man or the bird
who treats reflection as the enemy
it is?

Solitude, a Math Problem

A lone horse is never alone.
It's friends with the ground and the sky
sits on its back. Water is never alone.
Even a single drop, in seeming a lost child
of rain, brings reunion, flowers, umbrellas,
floods to mind, and in the action
of those thoughts, their gathering
out of hiding places, there is friction,
warmth. It has always seemed to her
that without her face she'd have been rain
or a horse, without the solitude
of the particular, the general shapelessness
would embrace her, that once born,
she was bound to look at light
and Pluto and blood
as no one else did: a castaway.
Despite the industry of her hiding
and pursuit, despite every pill,
drink, fuck, cut, prayer—
she has lived the birth
of a noun, the fuckcutprayer—behind
and around and within the atlas of her days,
there has been a constant turning away
of a small and unseen face, the locket
of the self, a loneliness so deep

as to refute its own eyes, making her wonder:
who am I accountable to, who is writing
all this down, who keeps knocking
over the vases and letting tornadoes in
to have their way with the decor?
Other people are little help. A kiss, yes
awhile, same with a fuck, a bite, a yell,
a smile, a knife, a sigh.
But two times "I don't know"
is "We don't know"
and a thousand times worse.

What from the Outside Seems Whim from the Inside
Goes by *Avalanche*

How do cats make up their minds?
I will lie here an hour or ten minutes
then go there and lie there an hour
or ten minutes. I will lick my paws
I will lick my tail. I will stop
licking my paws I will stop
licking my tail and stick my leg out
and hold it while staring at nothing
happening by the fence post.
Before before before she killed herself
she was washing dishes. Before before
she killed herself she called a friend
in Paris and talked of the flooding
in Venice. Before she killed herself
she watered the plants. Her fingers
had soil on them as she went down
the stairs. I will stand by the window
and cry I will sit on the toilet
and pretend I will never cry again.
I will take all the yellow pills I
will take all the green pills I
will take all the yellow and green pills
and flush them. I will stab my uterus
with a knitting needle I will fill

my uterus with lava I will admit
my uterus is an excuse. I will want
to vanish when I am seven when I am
wet when I am arranging flowers when
I am laughing at men for running
with the bulls when I am fucking
when I am hitting a bell with a hammer
when I am dreaming I have shoes
for hands when I am putting a noose
around my neck and finally finally
feeling that I am standing before
the right door. All those plants are dead.

Space Travel

A long looking at his looking at the window

Light leaving last from the bottom of the day,
shadows spreading like water between trees, a lake
his mind dives, comes back with a fish on a spear

There's a formula for how far horizon, simple,
she remembers that quality but not the facts:

take your height, add the number of times
you were warned of bear in Alaska, the number of hours
you spent in closets as a child, painting with
and on the dark, leading to a figure
and woman who can't survive
division by zero

Then he turns and smiles and she smiles

Teeth bright in the last light the day has on its mind

Little suns practically speaking, stars to navigate by,
ten feet of breathing between them, the gravity
of the body and the past, a few steps:

light-years

Real Love

Last night a cow sound
ed stabbed in throat or eye
down by the river wheezing thorns
of shrieks in his ears

he knew an angel was cutting
the cow's heart free
spreading blood on wings
flying red over fields
toward her sleep and still
stood naked doing nothing
bits of snow in the air
with moonlight and star as if
a child's drawing of Christmas
es future had been ripped
off a fridge and told to get
a real job

why did not he warn her
his love was the shadow
of a bloody wing and save her
the bother of him
when they met by turning
into a sliver of cedar
in her hand time alone
would remove without her
lifting a finger or scream?

The Meet-Cute (a Pagedream)

You have a zit.

(He touches his nose.) It makes me feel seventeen.

God I remember waking to a zit and thinking my life was over.

Did you like popping them?

Yes. Especially earlobe zits. They sounded like tiny squishy carrots being snapped.

I don't think you belong anywhere near salad. Maybe Stalin's salad, but not mine.

What would you put in Stalin's salad?

Don't know. This is only the second time it's come up tonight.
Ares asked earlier (points at small statue on a bookcase).
Kale. Arugula, though that sounds more like a language
than a green. Tenpenny nails. Little bits of Hitler.

Dictator for the dictator.

How do you know Becka?

She and I lie about wanting to scuba dive in Aruba together.

The bonding of fictive rubber suits.

Something like that. The chance to say "scuba in Aruba"
should never be passed up. Saying it feels like hopscotching.
How do you know Becka?

I don't. I just heard that woman over there say her name.
I don't know anyone here. I was walking by, the door was open,
I heard "Take Five" and thought, If I have a soul,
I should be able to walk into that house, hold a glass of red wine,
and talk with people about the death of the book.

The book is dead?

The book is ash. The book is a shadow of T.S. Eliot's
sexual frustration.

Someone always wanted to be a librarian. I love reading.
I'm reading right now. I'm always reading.
Turning the pages of your face. Dog-earing
the way you smiled when you lied about that
being Ares.

It's not Ares? I thought that was Ares. But I think all
Greek-looking statues at parties full of people
I don't know are Ares. How do you dog-ear a face?

(She taps the side of her head.) Lovingly. And if you don't
have a soul?

I guess I'd cry. I don't know what you mean.

You said before, If I have a soul, I should be able to drink
too much wine and be wrong about art, or something
like that. Do you think about the soul often?

(He does a version of a dance he saw Christopher Walken do once
in a music video, a dance he thinks about every few months,
a dance he later learned was improvised, as everything is,
even the sun every day, a dance of a million volts, of a hawk
opening a diary and writing on page one: I will come back
as the sky.)

Is that a measure of the frequency or the intensity with which
you think of the soul?

I wish I knew.

It was lovely. I think it got Ares's attention. Look: he's tapping
a toe. I think the soul has a closet full of capes
for all occasions. The cape of hiding from the moon.
The cape of wishing you could recall your mother's face.
I like capes. They're coats for people with wings.

Do you wear capes?

I have never worn a cape. The cape is perfect in my thoughts,
just like the soul has never got lost in Chicago or cheated
on its taxes. The soul is the wish to do better. "Take Five"
is a good song.

"Take Five" is a great song.

It should be "Take Six."

"Take Infinity."

Oh my, Mr. Wolf, what big pockets you have.

What's your name?

You know, I don't have one of those. My parents couldn't decide.

What do people call you?

Klutzy. Fleeting. Difficult. Seldom. I like my privacy.
There's nothing like a closet in a room in a room
in a room in a house in a cave in a book on a shelf
in a room in a room in a room in a house
in someone's head.

Kind of like this.

Exactly like this.

Now We're Not Getting Somewhere

All of them together once. Dinner once. Anna
and Stephanie and them. Three women
one man. Three and a half women
one half man. Describe the night:

The lifting of a flat stone up a hill.
The working of it to your thighs,
then to standing, then the flop over
and again, again. Is love momentum and this

entropy? Is entropy the triumph
of nostalgia, the big homecoming game?

Goodnight goodnight goodnight goodnight.

Anna and Stephanie went here, there,
while they went home to drink Molotov cocktails
as the plane went down.

I love you drunk in a sober mood.

Like putting a tux on to fight a fire.

The elegance of their marriage:
Do you take this man/woman
to be your lawfully wedded accident
to not flee the scene of?

I did/I shouldn't have/I would
again, again.

A Natural Theory of Suicide

If a tree could
it would walk
to the best sun

       (and if it could not)

the flattest ground

       (and if it could not)

the sweetest birds

       (and if it could not)

the most honest horizon

       (and if it could not)

the fewest axes
the quietest saws

       (and if it could not)

       (if it leaned to the left)

       (if diseased: ash borers)

(if lightning: I am half the reaching
I used to be)

(and if hands)

(if wise as trees seem to be)

would it pick up

    (it would)

and point

    (if head)

where

    (head)

if what

    (gun)

Used Book, Omen

It took ten years before he noticed
someone had stabbed his Ovid hard.

The last word the blade touched: *thirsty.*

To get to *thirsty* it traveled through *temple,*
serpent, went, waist, woman, garments, crimson,
shadow, on, of, to, the, then, a, my, comrades, wonder,
gone, sorrow, torture, earth, stood, healing,
better, compliment, heard, morning—an incomplete list.

In a testing mood he asks every living person
what they think of this: That's nice, they all say.

What his wife had said: You have to write a story
using only the words chosen by the knife's anger.

A crimson shadow, healing by better compliment,
garments a woman in wonder and sorrow.

A crimson woman, in garments of wonder and sorrow,
compliments the earth.

A gone woman, a crimson sorrow, a serpent shadow,
comrades: my garments of torture.

Woman gone: shadow torture. Then stood morning,
a healing garment of better wonder.

Did She Leave a Suicide Image?

When it came I could see it coming.
A dead oak that walked out of the horizon
to stuff brown leaves in my heart.
Dry blood in my speech and kiss.
A sharp rustling in my eyes.   Another

way to autopsy my spirit is tar. Touch it
and be me. Drink it and wait for the infection
of shadow, an ooze behind or in front,
depending on the accusation
of the sun.   Another

time I took all these pills I won't bore you
with the ancestry of, in the company of horses
and the accoutrements of horses, grass
and wind and flies and standing tall and
still : : : : a lake found
and filled me, I was the supporting water
below and the top water hosannaed up,
until someone saved me from being
saved.   Another

way to think of pumping my stomach
is theft.   The meticulous

way to paint me from the inside out: crush maggots
and dip your brush.

A Recipe

He was she was they was knife. (and water) They was a guitar
played by fire. (and water) She was purple loosestrife.
(and water) He was slag. (and water) They was night
touching blackout windows devoured by blackout drunk.
(and water)

During one of her gones he woke to an apple on her pillow.
She had perigeed. Slipped in. Had been whisper-handed.
Cloud across floor. Rain falling home.

Once a man who sometimes wanted to kill himself
loved a woman who sometimes wanted to live. She was flood
he was puddle. She was ocean he was tide. They was trickle
wave drown. The world makes us and ever after
drinks us back: his feel on the subject of the All.
Unholdable God the voice in our rivering flesh begging
Hold me.

Gone

He passes steam
climbing the ladder of itself.
A metal man
on a metal horse
from a rusted war.
Manuscripts of windows.
If I do not turn around,
the horse is now riding the man.
Full moon, high tide.
The water of him sits
higher in his thoughts.
His thoughts sit higher
in his head. He is living
a few inches above himself.
An hour of walking, two.
A good flâneur is deadtired
by the time he walks up
behind himself, asks,
Have we met? No.
I have me confused
with someone else.

Stride for Stride

Anna is good to him. *Shhhh* **was the first word.**
He wants to tell her everything. **They have dug
in Sumer and found this, the first song,
the only true version of God.** To tell her everything
would mean he knows everything, including the sounds
of its faces. **He will write the *Book of Hush Now.***
Otherwise how speak? **Send his mouth to the School
of the Empty Ear.** Anna is good to him. **For what is
what we say?** He wants to tell her something.
Breath through the larynx's reed? To tell her something
would mean he is keeping secrets. **The fallen petal
of a bloom?** That there is a cave in him. **Dog
with a bone?** Paintings on the walls. **Dog
with a bone.** The testament of reaching
from ochered hands. **We are always at least two.**
Anna is good to him. **The river of being
and its naysayer.** He wants to tell her nothing.
You call that a flood? If he starts talking
about his wife he will never stop. **Consciousness
and its intuitive dreaming of lobotomy.** He
will become waterfall, one hundred percent mouth.
What wolf critiques its fangs? It would take a novel
to speak of the shadow of her kiss on the back
of his neck, to hold how he remembers the noose
as his hands around her throat. **What star asks,**

Why am I on fire and running from the womb
of it all? Anna is good to him. To get the attention
of silence, we make noise. He will live with her
as an orrery of her motions, will rain and echo,
crash. But silence is too polite to say, I'm sorry,
I wasn't listening.

ABOUT THE AUTHOR

Bob Hicok has received a Guggenheim and two NEA Fellowships, the Bobbitt Prize from the Library of Congress, nine Pushcart Prizes, and was twice a finalist for the National Book Critics Circle Award. His poems have been selected for inclusion in nine volumes of *The Best American Poetry*.

Poetry is vital to language and living. Since 1972, Copper Canyon Press has published extraordinary poetry from around the world to engage the imaginations and intellects of readers, writers, booksellers, librarians, teachers, students, and donors.

WE ARE GRATEFUL FOR THE MAJOR SUPPORT PROVIDED BY:

academy of american poets

 ART WORKS.

 National Endowment for the Arts arts.gov

Lannan

amazon *literary partnership* ➤

 WASHINGTON STATE ARTS COMMISSION

THE PAUL G. ALLEN FAMILY FOUNDATION

 OFFICE OF ARTS & CULTURE SEATTLE

the point envision·enact·evolve

 CULTURE

 The Witter Bynner Foundation for Poetry

Richard Andrews and Colleen Chartier
Anonymous (2)
Jill Baker and Jeffrey Bishop
Anne and Geoffrey Barker
Donna Bellew
Matthew Bellew
Will Blythe
John Branch
Diana Broze
John R. Cahill
Sarah Cavanaugh
Keith Cowan and Linda Walsh
Stephanie Ellis-Smith and Douglas Smith
Mimi Gardner Gates
Gull Industries Inc. on behalf of William True
William R. Hearst III
Carolyn and Robert Hedin
David and Jane Hibbard
Bruce S. Kahn
Phil Kovacevich and Eric Wechsler
Lakeside Industries Inc. on behalf of Jeanne Marie Lee
Maureen Lee and Mark Busto

Peter Lewis and Johnna Turiano
Ellie Mathews and Carl Youngmann as The North Press
Larry Mawby and Lois Bahle
Hank and Liesel Meijer
Jack Nicholson
Petunia Charitable Fund and adviser Elizabeth Hebert
Madelyn S. Pitts
Suzanne Rapp and Mark Hamilton
Adam and Lynn Rauch
Emily and Dan Raymond
Joseph C. Roberts
Jill and Bill Ruckelshaus
Cynthia Sears
Kim and Jeff Seely
Nora Hutton Shepard
Arthur Sze
D.D. Wigley
Joan F. Woods
Barbara and Charles Wright
In honor of C.D. Wright, from Forrest Gander
Caleb Young as C. Young Creative
The dedicated interns and faithful volunteers of Copper Canyon Press

TO LEARN MORE ABOUT UNDERWRITING COPPER CANYON PRESS TITLES, PLEASE CALL 360-385-4925 EXT. 103

The pressmark for Copper Canyon Press
suggests entrance, connection, and interaction
while holding at its center
an attentive, dynamic space for poetry.

This book is set in Sabon.
Book design by Phil Kovacevich.
Printed on archival-quality paper.